FASCINATING
MILITARY SUBMARINES

by Kristin Marciniak

Content Consultant
Mitchell A. Yockelson
Adjunct Faculty
US Naval Academy

Core Library

An Imprint of Abdo Publishing
www.abdopublishing.com

www.abdopublishing.com

Published by Abdo Publishing, a division of ABDO, PO Box 398166, Minneapolis, Minnesota 55439. Copyright © 2015 by Abdo Consulting Group, Inc. International copyrights reserved in all countries. No part of this book may be reproduced in any form without written permission from the publisher. Core Library™ is a trademark and logo of Abdo Publishing.

Printed in the United States of America, North Mankato, Minnesota
092014
012015

Cover Photo: Mass Communication Specialist 3rd Class Adam K. Thomas/ US Navy
Interior Photos: Mass Communication Specialist 3rd Class Adam K. Thomas/US Navy, 1; Mike Hoffmann, 4; Micool Brooke/AP Images, 7; Ben Margot/AP Images, 8; Lieutenant Commander F.M. Barber, 12; akg-images/Newscom, 15; US Naval Historical Research Center, 18; AP Images, 20; Library of Congress, 22; US Navy, 26, 43; Ric Hedman, 28, 45; Mass Communication Specialist 2nd Class Jeremy Starr/US Navy, 33; Mass Communication Specialist 2nd Class Ricardo J. Reyes/US Navy, 36

Editor: Patrick Donnelly
Series Designer: Becky Daum

Library of Congress Control Number: 2014944241

Cataloging-in-Publication Data
Marciniak, Kristin.
 Fascinating military submarines / Kristin Marciniak.
   p. cm. -- (Ready for military action)
ISBN 978-1-62403-651-4 (lib. bdg.)
Includes bibliographical references and index.
1. Submarines (Ships)--United States--Juvenile literature.   I. Title.
623.825--dc23

                                            2014944241

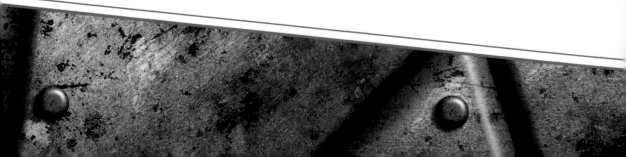

CONTENTS

CHAPTER ONE

ATTACK AND RESCUE

Fifteen British and Australian soldiers clung to a makeshift raft bobbing in the South China Sea. The men had no food or freshwater. They also had no shelter from the sun and saltwater. There was little chance of rescue.

It was September 14, 1944. Three days earlier, three US submarines had destroyed a convoy of Japanese ships and an oil tanker. It was the height of

Now docked in San Francisco Bay, the *Pampanito* took part in a dramatic rescue mission during World War II.

World War II (1939–1945). The United States and its allies, including the United Kingdom and Australia, needed to stop Japan at any cost. Their strategy included attacking ships that carried supplies such as fuel, food, and weapons.

The USS *Pampanito* and USS *Sealion* sank two Japanese merchant ships. But the US sailors didn't realize what kind of cargo the ships were carrying. On the ships were 2,200 prisoners of war (POWs) from the United Kingdom and Australia. Those 15 men on the raft were among the survivors.

The Bridge on the River Kwai

The 2,200 POWs aboard the Japanese merchant ships had survived the building of the bridge over the River Kwai. They were used as slave labor and treated terribly. The bridge was part of the "Railway of Death" that connected Bangkok, Thailand, and Rangoon, Burma. More than 100,000 men died during construction. Some died from starvation and tropical diseases. Others were overworked or beaten to death.

Tourists can now visit the bridge built by British and Australian POWs over the River Kwai.

A Brutal Captivity

The 2,200 POWs had been captives for three years. They spent 16 months in forced labor building a bridge in Southeast Asia. They barely made it out alive. Now they were being shipped to Japan to work in copper mines. As they floated through the wreckage they wondered if it would be worse to die on the open ocean or be worked to death by the Japanese. Some of the prisoners had already decided they didn't want to wait to find out. They threw themselves into the sea and drowned.

After three days at sea, the POWs spotted something in the water. Thirst and exhaustion had

The *Pampanito* was restored and is now open for tours in San Francisco, California.

caused some of them to hallucinate, or see things that were not really there. But the hulking submarine coming toward them was definitely real. It was the *Pampanito*. It was coming back to see if any of the Japanese ships were still afloat. The crew was astonished to find the raft of 15 POWs, as well as dozens of other soldiers floating in the ocean.

A Risky Decision

The *Pampanito* crew sprang into action. They hoisted the 15 weary POWs aboard the submarine. Then they went back to find more survivors. It was a dangerous task. Japanese fighter planes or warships could appear at any moment. But the sailors were dedicated to saving as many men as possible.

The *Pampanito* rescued 73 POWs from the shipwreck. The submarine already had 79 enlisted men and 10 officers on board. The crew wanted to keep searching for survivors, but there just wasn't room on the sub. Other allied submarines changed course to help rescue more of the remaining survivors. A total of 160 soldiers were rescued, including those picked up by the *Pampanito*. A typhoon blew into the South China Sea soon after, ending the search for any last survivors.

Once it had taken aboard as many POWs as it could hold, the *Pampanito* started its long journey to the US base on the Pacific island of Saipan. For six days, the crew cared for the gravely ill POWs. Many had malaria, diarrhea, and sores on their skin. All of them suffered from malnutrition. Crew members gave up their bunks, shared their clothing, and helped feed the rescued soldiers.

Submarines are often seen as machines of war. But the crew of the *Pampanito* showed that these underwater vessels are more than just weapons. They are research stations, stealth observation vehicles, and the homes of tightly knit crews serving their country. A few hours before, the POWs faced certain death. Thanks to the crew of the *Pampanito*, they had another chance at life.

Explore the *Pampanito*

The USS *Pampanito* was put into service six times during World War II. Today, the ship is a historic landmark located at Fisherman's Wharf in San Francisco, California. Maritime historians are restoring the *Pampanito*. They want it to look and work just like it did back in 1945. Visitors can climb aboard and experience life on a World War II submarine. Visitors can even stay overnight for a hands-on science sleepover. They can build a mini-sub, make a periscope, and construct a battery with actors playing the crew of the *Pampanito*.

The following passage is from an interview with K. L. Reulou. He was an Australian soldier and POW rescued by the *Pampanito* and its crew. He describes what he felt and saw as the *Pampanito* came into view:

> That afternoon between four and five the marvelous and wonderful thing happened. A submarine was making straight for us but we did not know to whom it belonged. My eyes were paining with oil and I could not see so clearly but when it was right opposite I saw a couple of men with machine guns pointing them at us. I didn't care because it would have been a quicker way out and believe me they looked tough, but instead of lead we got a rope and was taken aboard. Can you imagine the shock we got?

Source: Robert Bennet. "POW Survivor Tales and Robert Bennet Diary." USS Pampanito. San Francisco Maritime National Park Association, n. d. Web. Accessed August 11, 2014.

Point of View

After reading Reulou's account of the rescue, go back and reread the corresponding section of Chapter One. What new information does his story provide? What information is missing? Which account is more interesting to read? Which is more informative? Write a short essay comparing the two descriptions of the rescue.

Fig. 2.

CHAPTER TWO

ORIGINS OF THE SUBMARINE

Submarines might seem like exclusively modern ships. But they actually date back to ancient times. The first submarine belonged to Alexander the Great, a Greek king. It was built in 333 CE and looked nothing like the submarines of today. It was more like a glass diving bell. The king used it to observe animal life in the Aegean Sea.

The diving bell was one of the first diving chambers invented.

Artist and inventor Leonardo da Vinci was also interested in submarines. In 1515 he drew plans for a submersible boat. The boat had a wood frame covered by waterproof goatskins. It was to be propelled by wooden oars. Da Vinci never tested his design. In fact, it took another 100 years for the first working submarine to be tested in the Thames River in England. It was propelled by oars and stayed underwater for three hours.

The Diving Bell

A diving bell is just what it sounds like: a large bell-shaped container used for going underwater. The diver stands on top of a platform connected to the open bottom by cables. The bell is lowered straight down into the water. Air is trapped inside. The diver stays mostly dry and can safely breathe.

The Turtle

The first military submarine belonged to the United States. It was built in 1776 for use against the British during the American Revolution (1775–1783). It was named the *Turtle*, but it actually looked more like an egg. It was made of

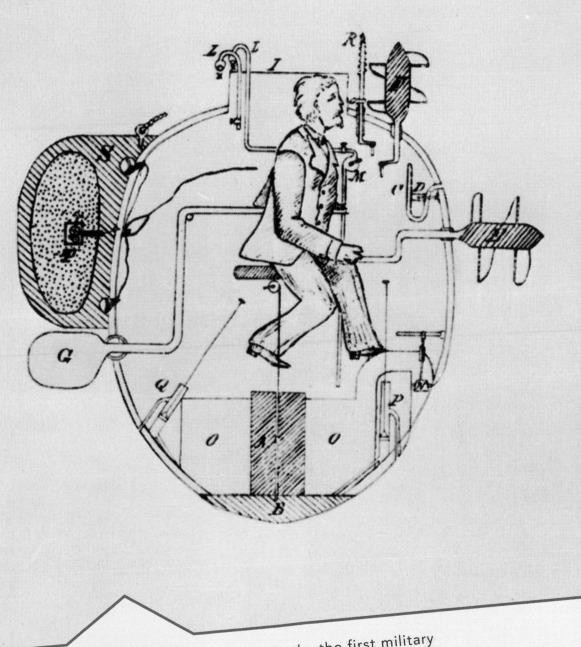

An interior sketch of the *Turtle*, the first military submarine.

The Science of Sinking

The *Turtle* was built on the principle of buoyancy. To submerge, the operator let water into the ship's ballast tanks. Ballast tanks are compartments inside the boat that can be filled with water or air. This extra water made the boat heavy and it sank. When the water was pumped out, the boat became lighter and rose to the surface.

Today's submarines also have ballast tanks. Water is let into the tanks when the sub needs to sink. When it's time to rise, water is pumped out and air is pushed in. To stay underwater at a specific depth, the crew balances the weight of the water and air in the ballast tanks.

oak. Its operator rotated a hand crank that turned a propeller. It held only 30 minutes of oxygen. Sergeant Ezra Lee was supposed to propel the tiny boat behind a warship, then dive underwater. A drill bit on the outside of the *Turtle* would attach a waterproof bomb to the warship.

It didn't work. Despite several attempts, Lee couldn't get the bomb to attach to the enemy ship. The British chased Lee and his tiny submersible boat back to shore.

Military submarines have changed a lot since the American Revolution. David Bushnell, the creator of the *Turtle*, described his invention in a letter to Thomas Jefferson in 1787:

> *The inside was capable of containing the operator, and air, sufficient to supply him, thirty minutes, without receiving fresh air. At the bottom, opposite to the entrance, was fixed a quantity of lead for ballast. At one edge, which was directly before the operator, who sat upright, was an oar, for rowing forward or backward. At the other edge, was a rudder for steering. An aperture, at the bottom, with its valve, was designed to admit water for the purpose of descending; & two brass forcing pumps served to eject the water within, when necessary for ascending. At the top, there was likewise an oar, for ascending or descending, or continuing at any particular depth.*

Source: "The Submarine *Turtle*: Naval Documents of the Revolutionary War." The Navy Department Website. *US Navy, n. d. Web. Accessed August 11, 2014.*

Consider Your Audience

Review this passage closely. Write a brief paragraph conveying the information from Bushnell's letter. Adapt the information to fit into Chapter Five alongside the descriptions of today's submarines. Remember to consider your audience and their interests. How does your new approach differ from the original text? Why?

CHAPTER THREE

SUBMARINES IN BATTLE

It was almost 100 years after the *Turtle* before a submarine suited for battle was built. During the American Civil War (1861–1865) the South, or Confederacy, fought the North, or Union. In 1863 a Confederate officer designed a submersible boat named the *H. L. Hunley*. It carried eight men. Like the *Turtle*, the *Hunley* was driven by a hand-cranked propeller. A long rod attached to the front of the boat

Confederate submarine *H. L. Hunley*

Inventor John P. Holland poses in the hatch of the submarine the US Navy purchased from him in 1900.

carried a torpedo. The crew rammed the torpedo into the side of an enemy ship, causing an explosion.

The *Hunley* wasn't easy to use. It sank three times during early tests. All three crews died. When the *Hunley* entered the war in 1864, it sank the Union warship *Housatonic*. Unfortunately, the *Hunley* sank too. Still, it was a victory for the Confederacy.

Improvements were needed, but the *Hunley* proved that submarines could be useful in combat.

The *Holland*

The US Navy purchased its first submarine in 1900. It was designed by John P. Holland, the winner of a submarine design contest held by the navy. The USS *Holland* was actually his sixth design. It was 53 feet (16.2 m) long and weighed 63 short tons (57.2 metric tons). It carried six sailors and three self-propelled torpedoes. It also had a gun on top of the boat for attacking or defending

Building a Better Sub

The *Holland* and other submarines of its era ran on gasoline. Electric batteries let them submerge for short periods of time. The gas engines recharged the batteries when the boats surfaced. Gasoline engines aren't very safe. Gasoline is very flammable. Diesel fuel is safer because it's more stable. So in 1911, the United States built its first diesel-powered submarine. The diesel engine created steam. The steam turned turbines, creating electricity for heating, powering, and lighting the submarine. But diesel engines need oxygen to work, so the boats still had to use batteries underwater.

A German U-boat stranded on the south coast of England after it had surrendered during World War I

when it wasn't submerged. The *Holland* traveled at six knots, or approximately seven miles per hour (11 km/h). It could sink 75 feet (23 m) deep.

The *Holland* never saw battle. Submarine technology improved rapidly over the next decade. That made the navy's 1900 purchase seem practically ancient. The *Holland* was retired in 1910, making way for new, more advanced boats. Diesel engines replaced gasoline ones. Periscopes and torpedoes were updated to be stealthier and more accurate.

New wireless technology let submersible boats communicate with bases on shore. All of these additions were soon tested in battle.

War on the Water

Early in World War I (1914–1918) Germany began using submarines to stop ships from delivering weapons and food to British troops. The Germans planned on winning the war by starving the British.

The Germans also used their submarines to terrorize civilians. International law said that military vessels had to warn civilian ships before firing. Germany ignored that law in 1915 and fired on the *Lusitania*, a British ocean liner. The *Lusitania* sank. Nearly 2,000 people onboard died, including 123 Americans. Protests at home led to the United States joining the war as the United Kingdom's ally in 1917.

Submarine technology improved between World Wars I and II. The United States and the United Kingdom built additional submarines that protected their fleets from enemy vessels. Torpedoes were

U-Boats

Germany's Unterseeboots, also known as U-boats, were some of the deadliest weapons used in World War I and World War II. At the end of World War I, the Treaty of Versailles banned Germany from owning submarines. Adolf Hitler, who came to power in Germany in the 1930s, ignored that law. He rebuilt Germany's submarine fleet stronger than before. After World War II the United States and its allies split up the remaining U-boats to study how they were built and why they were so effective.

equipped with magnetic fuses. Instead of requiring impact with an enemy ship, torpedoes could now explode when they came within range of the ship's magnetic field. The newer models also used sonar and radar to locate enemy ships.

The improvements paid off. Submarines made up less than 2 percent of the US Navy in World War II (1939–1945), but they sank more than 30 percent of Japan's navy. They also destroyed 5 million short tons (4.5 million metric tons) of enemy supplies. But it wasn't all good news for the United States and its allies. More than 3,500 sailors died on 52 sunken submarines.

Submarines simply weren't built to stay underwater. They spent approximately 90 percent of their time above water, taking in oxygen for their diesel engines and motoring to the next battleground. They dove underwater only long enough to attack or hide from the enemy. Once underwater, their electric batteries limited the boat's speed. Another power source was needed, and fast.

EXPLORE ONLINE

The website below has even more information about early submarines. As you know, every source is different. Reread Chapter Three of this book. What are the similarities between Chapter Three and the information you found on the website? Are there any differences? How do the two sources present information differently?

Office of Naval Technology
www.mycorelibrary.com/submarines

CHAPTER FOUR

A CHANGING SUBMARINE PROGRAM

The end of World War II brought the United States a new enemy. The Soviet Union was an ally during the war, but the United States saw its fleet of more than 300 submarines as a threat. The US military wanted more information about what the Soviets were doing. But it didn't want to anger its former ally, so any reconnaissance mission had to be secret.

A submarine's snorkel lets in fresh air for the engines while allowing the sub to stay underwater.

The USS *Gudgeon*

Fortunately, the US Navy's submarine force was becoming stealthier all the time. After World War II it experimented with a large snorkel like the ones on German U-boats. The snorkel let in fresh air for the diesel engines. Now boats could recharge their electric batteries with just the snorkel poking out of the water.

Spies in the Deep

The navy also manned submarines with spies. Known as spooks, they were trained to monitor Soviet military signals and communication above and below water. Spooks listened to Soviet military radio frequencies. They also listened for sonar and radar pings. If they heard pings it meant the submarine was in danger of being found and had to dive.

Diesel submarines eventually had to come up for air to recharge batteries and take in fresh oxygen for the crew. In 1957 the USS *Gudgeon* was snorkeling just a few miles from Soviet shores when it was spotted by

Soviet Submarine Panic

Many in the United States feared the Soviet Union in the 1950s. Stories about Soviet submarines along US shores were common. One person even falsely reported a spy submarine in a Texas lake that was only five feet (1.5 m) deep. In reality Soviet submarines couldn't get close to the United States. The only route was through a gap between Greenland, Iceland, and the United Kingdom that was closely guarded.

two enemy ships. It immediately dove, but it was too late. More Soviet ships arrived on the scene. The *Gudgeon* was trapped. The boat had already been submerged for 12 hours. The batteries were drained. The air inside was heavy and becoming toxic. After a two-day standoff, the *Gudgeon* was forced to surface for the safety of the crew.

When the *Gudgeon* reached the surface, it was greeted by three small Soviet ships. The *Gudgeon*'s crew identified themselves and said they were going back to Japan. The Soviets let them go.

Going Nuclear

The *Gudgeon*'s forced surfacing was a major defeat for the United States. The navy needed a submarine that could stay underwater for long periods of time without a snorkel. The answer was nuclear power. The USS *Nautilus*, built in the early 1950s, was the first nuclear-powered submarine. It didn't need a snorkel to bring oxygen to the crew. It actually made the oxygen.

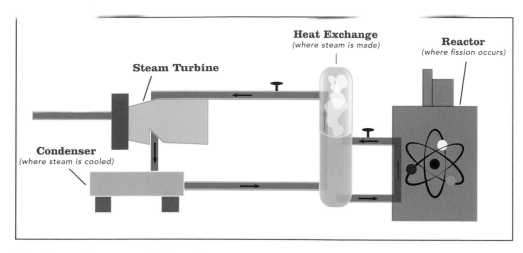

Nuclear-Powered Engine

This diagram shows how a nuclear-powered submarine engine works. How does the information presented in the text compare to the information in the diagram? Has the diagram changed your understanding of the nuclear process?

How It Worked

In a nuclear-powered engine, uranium atoms are split in a process called fission. That split produces heat. The heat turns water to steam. Steam turns the turbines. Turning turbines create power. That power is used to propel the boat. It also runs machines that clean the air and make oxygen and water for the crew.

The *Nautilus* could stay underwater for months or years at a time. The only limitation was how much food it could carry for the crew. It was faster than diesel-powered submarines, moving at 23 knots, or 26 miles per hour (42 km/h), both on the surface and underwater. It was quieter than a diesel submarine too. The navy had finally created a stealthy submarine.

Anatomy of a Submarine

There are four kinds of US military submarines in use today. They are attack submarines (SSN), ballistic-missile submarines (SSBN), guided-missile submarines (SSGN), and the Submarine Rescue Diving and Recompression System (SRDRS). With the exception of the SRDRS, all military submarines have the same general design.

The pressure hull is where the sailors live and work. It's the main body of the submarine. The main ballast tanks are outside the pressure hull. They are located near the bow, or front of the boat. Inside the bow is the submarine's sonar equipment. At the opposite end of the boat is the stern. That's where the screw is located. The screw is a giant propeller that provides propulsion for the boat.

Crew members lower a 3,000-pound (1,361 kg) torpedo onto the USS *Frank Cable* during a training exercise.

Attack Submarines (SSN)

There are 54 SSNs in the US Navy's fleet. The SSN is fast, fierce, and deadly. True to its name, it's used for attacking enemy ships and ground targets. It's also used to gather information and deliver troops to dangerous areas. The SSNs are the shortest boats in the navy's fleet of submarines, falling between 353 and 453 feet (108 and 138 m) in length.

Ballistic- and Guided-Missile Submarines (SSBNs and SSGNs)

The navy owns 14 SSBNs. They use the threat of nuclear missiles, which are carried on board, to keep enemies from attacking US territory.

The navy also has four SSGNs, also known as "boomers." They handle land-attack missions and assist US Special Forces. SSGNs can carry up to 66 Special Forces personnel at a time. These soldiers and sailors can be deployed from the ship or brought inside to safety through special chambers. The chambers allow people to enter and exit the submarine while it is below the surface.

Each SSGN can carry up to 154 Tomahawk land cruise missiles. Empty missile tubes are used to carry equipment and food for longer trips to sea. They can even carry unmanned underwater and air vehicles.

Rescue Vehicles

The USS *Thresher* sank during tests off the coast of Massachusetts in 1963. The accident killed 129 sailors and shipyard workers, spurring the navy to design an underwater rescue vehicle. The Deep Sea Rescue Vehicle was commissioned in 1977 and retired in 2008. It was replaced by the SRDRS. This system includes the Falcon, a rescue vehicle that attaches to a number of different kinds of surface ships. This unmanned vehicle is operated remotely from the surface ship. It can be used to rescue as many as 16 people up to 2,000 feet below the water's surface.

What's in a Name?

All navy submarines and ships are given the prefix USS. It stands for United States Ship. That's followed by the vessel's name. Older attack submarines are named after cities, such as the USS *Los Angeles*. The new Virginia-class submarines are named after states, famous Americans, and retired classes of submarines. Ballistic-missile and guided-missile submarines are named after states.

LIFE AS A SUBMARINER

Submariners make up just 6 percent of US Navy employees. It takes a lot of hard work to earn a position on a submarine. Submarine crews are small. Each member needs to be an expert in his or her own job and know how to do everyone else's jobs too. This is especially important if an emergency arises on board. Whoever is closest to the location of the problem needs to react quickly so the rest of

Submarine crews are used to living and working in cramped spaces.

Earning Your Dolphins

The Dolphin pin is one of the three major warfare pins in the US Navy. To earn a Dolphin pin sailors must know how to operate the submarine and save it during an emergency. They must be experts in damage control, the ship's power systems, and auxiliary systems, such as plumbing and electricity. They must also be knowledgeable about the submarine's electronic equipment and navigation and combat systems. "Earning your Dolphins" is one of the biggest events in a submariner's life. It shows commitment to the submarine service and one's fellow sailors.

the submarine's systems remain stable.

Enlisted sailors work with the boat's engines, generators, and electronics. Each position has its own training that lasts three to six months. Enlisted sailors also go through six months of hands-on nuclear-power training. They learn how a naval power plant works and how to safely operate it.

Submarine officers are the leaders of the boat. Their duties include operating the nuclear reactor, taking care of the

Attack		
Class	Los Angeles	Seawolf	Virginia
# of Boats	41	3	10
Engine Type	Nuclear	Nuclear	Nuclear
Length	360 feet (110 m)	353 feet (108 m) to 453 feet (138 m)	377 feet (115 m)
Speed	25 knots (28 mph) (45 km/h)	25 knots (28 mph) (45 km/h)	25 knots (28 mph) (45 km/h)
Crew	143	140	134
Weapons	-Tomahawk missiles -MK-48 torpedoes	-Tomahawk missiles -MK-48 torpedoes	-Tomahawk missiles -MK-48 torpedoes

	Ballistic-Missile	Guided-Missile
Class	Ohio	Ohio
# of Boats	14	4
Engine Type	Nuclear	Nuclear
Length	560 feet (170 m)	560 feet (170 m)
Speed	20 knots (23 mph) (37 km/h)	20 knots (23 mph) (37 km/h)
Crew	155	159
Weapons	-Trident II missiles -MK-48 torpedoes	-Tomahawk missiles -MK-48 torpedoes

Comparing Submarines

This chart shows details about each type of submarine owned by the US Navy as of 2013. Compare this information to the information in the text. How do the chart and text differ? Why do you think the author decided to use a chart to show this information? How does it help you understand the differences between submarines?

Women in the Sub Service

Until recently, only men could serve on US submarines. There wasn't enough separate living space for men and women on the boats. In 2011 minor changes were made to six submarines so female officers could serve. By the end of 2013, 43 women served on US submarines.

weapons systems, and driving the submarine. Officers start their training at nuclear power school. Then they go to hands-on training. Next is officer training, followed by their first tour at sea.

Working and Living at Sea

Imagine living in a long, narrow house that's three stories tall. Your neighborhood is 800 feet (244 m) below the sea. Your home has no windows. Machinery hums in the background. And you share that house with 150 other people.

Living on a submarine is completely different from life on dry land. Underwater, submariners have an 18-hour day. They work for six hours, and then they have 12 hours off. This structure ensures that every part of the boat is staffed at all times while keeping the crew members from getting too tired.

The US Navy's submarines are high-tech machines designed to protect and defend the United States and its allies. They are used in both times of war and peace. They carry powerful weapons and equally powerful listening devices. But the most important cargo on any submarine is its crew. These men and women serve on land and below the sea, ensuring the safety of our oceans and shores.

FURTHER EVIDENCE

Chapter Five is about life as a submariner. What was one of the chapter's main points? What are some pieces of evidence in the chapter that support this main point? Check out the website at the link below. Find a quote from the website that supports the chapter's main point. Does this quote support an existing piece of evidence in the chapter, or does it add a new one?

Life on a Sub
www.mycorelibrary.com/submarines

Revenge in Japan

In 1944 the USS *Cavalla* was coming off lookout duty. Captain Herman J. Kossler spotted one of World War II's most infamous targets, the Japanese aircraft carrier *Shokaku*. The *Shokaku* played a big part in the bombing of the US base at Pearl Harbor, Hawaii, in 1941. US troops in the Pacific were eager to send it to the bottom of the ocean. The *Cavalla* did just that. Its crew fired four torpedoes, quickly followed by another two. Three explosions signaled a hit as the *Cavalla* dove for safety. The US submarine sustained enemy fire that damaged the hull and the boat's sound gear. But within two hours, the crew heard the unmistakable sounds of the Japanese ship breaking apart at the seams as it sank to the ocean floor. The aircraft carrier that had done so much damage to the United States had been destroyed.

Arctic Exploration

In August 1957 the USS *Nautilus* became the first submarine to perform an underwater exploration of the Arctic Circle. Very few people had traveled so far north. No one knew how thick the ice was or the depth of the Arctic Ocean. It was a dangerous mission, especially since the *Nautilus* was the US Navy's only nuclear submarine at the time. Nobody knew how it would do at sea for that long of a trip. Many navy officials feared that the submarine would never be seen or heard from again. Still, Captain William Anderson was determined to reach the North Pole. It took a few trips, but the captain and crew arrived at the geographic North Pole on August 3, 1958. Overall, the mission was an enormous success. The United States gained knowledge about the Arctic's underwater terrain. And the *Nautilus* proved that nuclear power was the future of the navy's submarine service.

The USS Cavalla

Underwater Spies

In 1971 the USS *Halibut* was tasked with a dangerous classified mission. It had to locate a bundle of telephone wires at the bottom of the Sea of Okhotsk just north of Japan. These wires were part of an undersea communication network used by the Soviets. By tapping into these cables, the United States would have access to Soviet military communications and planning. After a week of searching, the submarine's crew located the cable. It was buried underneath sand, surrounded by giant crabs and tiny jellyfish. Divers attached the tap, a recorder inside a small box, to the cable. The tap recorded words and data that went through the wires. Tapes from the tap were retrieved and analyzed. For the first time, the United States had an inside look into the operations of the Soviet Union.

Take a Stand

In Chapter One the sailors on the *Pampanito* rescued only 73 of the 2,200 POWs floating in the South China Sea. Do you agree with the captain's decision to stop the rescue effort? Should the sailors have gone against orders and continued pulling POWs aboard the sub? Write a short essay explaining your opinion. Make sure to give reasons for your opinion and details that support those reasons.

Why Do I Care?

It's interesting to learn about old-fashioned inventions, such as historic submarines. How have the previous versions of submarines impacted the submarines of today? What improvements were made? What improvements do you think will be made to modern nuclear submarines? Use your imagination and explain your answers.

Say What?

Studying submarines can mean learning a lot of new vocabulary. Find five words in this book that you have never heard before. Use a dictionary to find out what they mean. Then write the meanings in your own words. Use each word in a sentence.

Surprise Me

This book includes information about how the purpose of the US Navy's submarine service has changed over time. After reading this book, what two or three facts about the submarine service's duties did you find most surprising? Write a few sentences about each fact and explain why you found it surprising.

GLOSSARY

auxiliary
available to produce something extra or additional when needed

buoyancy
the power of a fluid to put an upward force on a body placed in it

maritime
having to do with the sea

periscope
an instrument that allows a submarine crew to see above the water's surface

propulsion
the forward motion of a body produced by a force

radar
equipment used to detect distant objects using radio waves

snorkel
a tube or tubes that can be extended above the surface of the water to supply air to and remove exhaust from a submerged submarine

sonar
a device that uses sound waves to detect submerged objects

stealth
intended not to attract attention

submerge
to put or go underwater

torpedo
a cylindrical, self-propelled submarine weapon that explodes when it contacts its target

LEARN MORE

Books

Cooke, Tim (Ed.). *Submarines (Ultimate Military Machines)*. Mankato, MN: Smart Apple Media, 2013.

Hamilton, John. *Submarines (Military Ships)*. Mankato, MN: Abdo Publishing, 2012.

Websites

To learn more about the US military and its resources, visit **booklinks.abdopublishing.com**. These links are routinely monitored and updated to provide the most current information available.

Visit **www.mycorelibrary.com** for free additional tools for teachers and students.

INDEX

ABOUT THE AUTHOR

Kristin Marciniak has a journalism degree from the University of Missouri–Columbia. She lives in Kansas City, Missouri, with her husband, son, and golden retriever.